WILL THE REAL KEANU REEVES PLEASE STAND UP?

Anne Mitchell

Will the Real Keanu Reeves Please Stand Up?

Copyright © *Anne Mitchell, 2024*

All Rights Reserved

This book is subject to the condition that no part of this book is to be reproduced, transmitted in any form or means, electronic or mechanical, stored in a retrieval system, photocopied, recorded, scanned, or otherwise. Any of these actions require the proper written permission of the author.

Dedicated to...Robert E. Mitchel, C.M.1

Table of Contents

Part One Chapter One Birth, Annie-Jane and James 6

Chapter Two Ted 11

Chapter Three The two Lauras 12

Chapter Four Robert Edward 14

Chapter Five Michelle 15

Chapter Six Anne 17

Chapter Seven Keanu 24

Chapter Eight The Homeless Woman 33

Chapter Nine Distraught and Heartbroken 34

Part Two THE WILL 36

Chapter Ten The Will 37

Part One

Chapter One

The night before I was born, my father did not have enough money to take a cab home to his and my mother's apartment, so he walked part of the way. There were no more buses in circulation because it was 3:00 a.m. in the morning.

When I was baptized, it was so warm outside that I got the priest sweat on my forehead not holy water…

Annie-Jane and James

This story goes back way back. It goes back to my ancestor, a German woman who was born in 1841 and died in 1921, and her name was Annie-Jane Shuller-Kraft. She came to Detroit, Michigan, when she was about 14 or 15 and pregnant. We are talking about a long way back, back when it was a great shame to be pregnant at that age, a time when they had to hide you if you were pregnant or you had to hide yourself.

She came looking for her aunt, who was living in the United States. She did not get along with her stepmother back in Germany. Her mother had died, and her father had remarried, and she did not like her new mom. Her uncle was the captain of a boat, so she left for America on his boat. When she arrived in the States, she looked for her aunt. The child died. She met a 30 year old French-Canadian man called Vénérand Baillageon in Detroit. They were later to be married. She lived to be 80 and raised 12 children. Rumor has it that when she came to Canada, or Québec to be more precise, she did not speak for two years, and when she finally did, she could speak French fluently.

About my great-great-grandfather on my father's side. He was sent to jail for participating in a demonstration and bearing arms so that working people could have the right to vote in England. Before those years, only the land owners had the right to vote there and perhaps in other parts of the world.

James Mitchell was married, with a young family, and became part of the Chartist movement.

From Wikipedia: From Wikipedia,

> **'Chartism** was a working-class movement for political reform in the United Kingdom that erupted from 1838 to 1857 and was strongest in 1839, 1842 and 1848. It took its name from the People's Charter of 1838 and was a national protest movement... The movement was fiercely opposed by government authorities, who finally suppressed it.
>
> The People's Charter called for six reforms to make the political system more democratic:
>
> *A vote for every man aged twenty-one years and above, of sound mind, and not undergoing punishment for a crime.*
>
> *The secret ballot to protect the elector in the exercise of his vote.*
>
> *No property qualification for Members of Parliament (MPs), to allow the constituencies to return the man of their choice.*
>
> *Payment of Members, enabling tradesmen, working men, or other persons of modest means to leave or interrupt their livelihood to attend to the interests of the nation.*
>
> *Equal constituencies, securing the same amount of representation for the same number of electors, instead of allowing less populous constituencies to have as much or more weight than larger ones.*
>
> *Annual parliamentary elections, thus presenting the most effectual check to bribery and intimidation, since no purse could buy a constituency under a*

system of universal manhood suffrage in every twelve months.'

'The recommendations were presented to a large group at a Chartist meeting in Stockport on July 26, 1839, attended by James Mitchell. The meeting was presided by Richard Polling who presented a motion to adopt the above recommendations. At the end of the motion, he predicted that if the Parliament were to accept the above recommendations, that would be the end of the rebellion, but that "the people must prepare themselves with arms, the great law authorities having held it legal to do so."

Mr. James Mitchell seconded the resolution.

Two weeks later James Mitchell and fifteen others were arrested and appeared before a magistrate. Policemen appeared as witnesses to events were the prisoners attended prohibited Chartist meetings. A reporter for a local newspaper, Edwin Hume, swore to the facts that Mitchell had expressed certain views at a public meeting in Newbridge-lane on May 11, 1839.

On August 9, 1839, James Mitchell received the following sentence:

> "*Mitchell,* committed to Chester Castle for conspiracy, sedition, attending unlawful meetings, seditious libels, and possession of firearms, and offensive weapons for an unlawful purpose."

'He and a fellow prisoner, Davies, were released on February 1841 on payment of bail, raised by their friends, and a promise not to disturb the peace for 5 years. On their release they were paraded to Chester and Liverpool by a large procession of Chartists, to finally arrive at home where a "Tea Festival" was held in their honour.

James Mitchell and his wife Emma gave birth to John Robert Mitchell, a Baptist minister, who, in turn with his wife Margaret, brought my grand-father Edward (Ted Mitchell), who emigrated to Canada in 1919.

Robert Edward Mitchell C.M., Ted's son and my dad, by luck has managed to date to stay out of prison.'

Chapter Two
Ted

My grandfather Edward, better known as Ted, left England at 19 to start a new life in Canada. Rumor has it he left because he was mad at his father, a Protestant minister—a man of the Church, a man of faith, and perhaps a rather strict figure. That's what my grandfather was leaving behind, or so I've come to believe.

Before emigrating, Ted had lied about his age to join the British Army, where he served as a bombardier during World War I. After the war, he made his way to Canada, drawn by the prospect of a fresh start. He had an uncle in Victoria, but apart from that family connection, he was alone in this new country. On the way to Victoria, he took up various odd jobs as he traveled, saving diligently so he could eventually experience the luxury of traveling First Class. When he was on his way to Québec and working at odd jobs so he could get there, he worked in Manitoba for a while with native (First Nations) people.

Then, he reached Québec and worked there, up north, in Val d'Or, in the Abitibi-Témiscamingue region. That is where he met my grandmother. She was working as a waitress in a hotel. They got married and raised three boys. My dad was the eldest of the three. My grandfather worked in mines in the Val-d'Or-Malartic region for most of his life. He was a master mechanic. He once was up for a promotion, and he did not get the job because his French was not good enough. Ted lived in Québec with my grandmother, my dad, and my uncles from 1937 to his death in 1973. He had not returned to England to visit his family for about 15 years after arriving in Canada. He received a letter from England with the news that his mother had passed away three months earlier.

Chapter Three

The Two Lauras

Both my grandmother's names were Laura. It was Marie-Laure and Laura. Marie-Laure Doyon was my maternal grandmother. She had been a school teacher in the *rangs* in Québec, which means a country school teacher, where every child in the village was in the same class regardless of age. When my grandfather met her, I think he thought she was a bit of a snob. She was from Beauce, and she was educated. He asked her if she wanted a drink, and she said no. So he told her she must not go to the bathroom very often.

She was a big woman, and she cooked with Crisco oil and made the best pancakes ever. She died at 90. She had a stroke and had developed Alzheimer's.

The other Laura was my paternal grandmother, Laura Gagnon. The name is so widespread in Québec, and they are probably all relatives. Her dream was to be an accountant, but she worked as a nanny and a maid. She also worked for the SAAQ and for a dentist for a little while after Ted passed away. Laura was the fifth in a family of 17 children. Her father was a blacksmith of 24 years old, and her mother was an 18-year-old schoolteacher when they got married. Her father, Isidore, was not rich, but he always spent money on doctors when his children were sick, so they all lived to be a certain age. They all survived illness when they were young. They lived through the great pandemic that was the Spanish flu.

When Laura was about ten years old, her friend got diphtheria and died. Laura got it, too, but she survived. She lived to be 87 years old. Her mother had all of her 17 children at home. She was one of the lucky ones because her father got her a doctor who came to help her and a close friend or family member. Other women were not so lucky, as you had to pay for health care in Canada in those days, and these ladies did not always have the means.

Christmases were more religious in those days in the French-Canadian society. Oranges were a luxury few people could afford, especially during the Great Depression. At Christmas, there were oranges in stores.

The Gagnon family celebrated Christmas by going to Midnight Mass and then eating a snack before everyone went to bed. There was always an older child who would stay home during Midnight Mass to care for the younger ones. The big celebrations were at New Year's. That is when everybody got presents.

Laura's brother died in Normandy in 1944 in WWII.

She met my grandfather (Ted) in 1937, and they were to be married for 36 years. It was not love at first sight for her. She had hoped for a tall, dark and handsome man. However, there was chemistry between them, and they were together until Ted's death. Laura said the two worst days of her life were when her dad died in 1931 and when her husband Ted died in 1973.

Ted was a Protestant. His father had been a Baptist pastor back in England, and he converted to Catholicism to marry Laura. He really had no choice because Laura's mother and her sister were not pleased about her marrying a Protestant. Catholics could not marry someone from another religion.

Chapter Four
Robert Edward

My dad was not the most serious student, but he was definitely a bright one. He was the class clown who later became wealthy. Once, a teacher even punched him in the stomach, and he passed out. He always challenged his teachers, getting himself into trouble, but he would always look up the answers to his questions himself in library documents.

He later joined the cadets and always dreamed of a career in the army or as a lawyer. He became a prominent patent agent and ended up getting the Order of Canada medal. He married my mother at 25 years old and stayed married to her for over 60 years. He also stayed with his firm for almost all of his life. He had worked in a print shop when he first arrived in Montréal.

Chapter Five

Michelle

My mother married my dad when she was 23. She was a stay-at-home mom who would have liked to further her education but never got the chance to since she became a mom and then a grandmother. When we were young, she took courses at the Conservatoire Lasalle, a French diction and elite theater school. It was a school of good quality in French-Canadian Montréal. She did not finish. I guess the fact that she had three daughters at home was a bit much for her. She always had the gift of writing, though. She was a good poet. She was curious and also enjoyed science. Her dad had died when my mother was 12 years old. She went to a Catholic Convent with nuns. It was an all-girls school. My mother has the fondest memories of her father, Honoré. She always remembers one time when he bought her a big, beautiful doll. Her sister told her she would get a cheap little doll. But when my grandfather got home, my mother saw her doll, and it was big and beautiful. She was so happy.

She also used to hide in the back of my grandfather's car because she wanted to go for a ride with him. Once he was far enough, she would pop out of the back, and he was too far to bring her back home. Once, she did not wait long enough to pop up, and he brought her back home. He told her: 'You should have waited a bit longer before you popped up', as he chuckled.

I later discovered that my grandfather never learned how to read or write. My grandmother handled his accounting, drawing on her experience as a schoolteacher, much like those in "Little House on the Prairie." Despite this challenge, my grandfather owned a sawmill, where he marked the lumber with ink, leaving my grandmother to count and organize it afterward.

Later in life, my grandfather was diagnosed with multiple sclerosis and became completely paralyzed for the last five years of his life.

During that time, he communicated solely through his eyes, opening and closing them to indicate yes or no.

Chapter Six
Anne

I was born on the wrong side of the tracks. My parents were quite poor when I was born. They used to take the bus down to Chinatown in Montréal for Chinese food on Sunday night. We lived in a small apartment on the poorer side of the tracks. We then moved into an apartment on the 'right' side of the tracks, then to a small house, where we lived until I was thirteen years old. My parents then bought a house that we would live in for forty years, adjacent to one of the wealthiest neighborhoods in Canada. I remember having a beautiful childhood, especially in the smaller house. We lived near a park. I was happy back then. We did not live in a big house, but we had a comfortable home with a big yard until I was about thirteen. We spent our summers at the cottage my mother inherited from her parents, which my father later bought. I used to spend so much time playing in the lake with my friend Suzanne. We would be in the water all day until our skin was like a prune.

I believe she liked my cousin Simon. I think she wanted to befriend me first to get close to Simon, which was fine with me. We were good friends; I might even say great friends. We used to write to each other when I was in Montréal in the winter and she was in Estrie. Simon used to ride his motorcycle on the country roads at the cottage where his father owned land. His father had money. They were not ultra-rich, but they were well off. I also remember picking currants in the country as a child. I would go with my aunts.

I have memories of my two cousins and I, Chloe and Mathilde, walking to the village. This was a long walk. We would go to the restaurant, have French fries and a Coke, and put quarters in the Jukebox for it to play our favorite songs. When my father and my uncle entered sailing races, we waited at the shore; Chloe, Mathilde I and played music on the jukebox and danced. People gave us quarters to play music on the jukebox and dance.

There were also memorable moments with my friend Gillian. At least in those days, she was a friend. We used to play on the swings at the park and go and watch softball games played by older men, also in the park. I can recall one year; we were both going to the same public school, and things were not good. I was being bullied by Gillian and her friends, and I was just not fitting into that school. My father even got a call one time from a teacher who said that I did not fit in that school with that crowd. One day, Gillian and a few other girls called me at home and invited me to join them at a restaurant. They then took me to the park and beat me up. When I was in elementary school, I remember Gillian being particularly mean along with this boy, Greg. I had curled my hair that day for school. They shoved my head in the snow, and I went home with no curls. That is besides the fact that she would later steal every boyfriend I had. I felt like she always had to have everything that I had.

Eventually, I just cut ties with her. I grew a distance between us and never saw her again.

When I was young, about seventeen, I had a boyfriend. His name was Steve. He was actually my first real love, as it stands out now, one of the three significant loves in my life. I also had a crush on this boy called Gabriel Branner. And here, I must mention my friend Gillian at the time, who, I will mention a bit later in this story, had "stolen" two of my boyfriends. Actually, she ended up marrying Steve.

I was and am a French Canadian and did all of my schooling in French, except for cégep, where I went to English school. That is where and when I had the most fun. Those were, apart from the last 2 1/2 years, the best years of my life, without a doubt. So, I was going out with a boy named Steve, and we had been going out for a couple of years. I loved him. We were engaged. He had had tragedy in his life. His mother had committed suicide when Steve was thirteen years old. His father had remarried, and he was living in the southern United States, South. He was an airline pilot. So, I was in love. We had a lot of fun.

We went to parties and had an active sex life and social life. Steve was half Jewish and half French Canadian. His mother was French Canadian. He was tall and skinny, dark, and not really handsome, but very sensual and sexy.

Then, I met James. James was shorter and blond, very skinny, and quite handsome. He was a Christian. I fell for him, too. I had gone to a beer bash one night at school. They were playing U2's New Year's Day, I remember. We necked, and French kissed. We had gone out for about one year when they both (Steve and James) showed up at my house for Valentine's Day. James had flowers. When he saw Steve there, he just rushed out and in what I can call anger. I tried to explain to him that I loved him, that Steve had shown up unexpectedly, but he would not listen and never tried to understand. One night, he came to my house. We had sex. Later, I found out I was pregnant. I was 19 years old. I knew the child was his, because I had not been with anyone else in that time period. I had not been with anyone else since I met him. I told him, and he left me anyway. He abandoned me, and I was pregnant. I guess I got my karma for leaving Steve.

I was in disarray and panicked. I did not know what to do. I asked my friend Belinda if she would come to the hospital with me to see if I could get an abortion. She came with me, and I did get an abortion. There was no way I would be able to raise a child by myself. I was in school. I was working part-time, but in those days, I was making minimum wage.

As it turned out, it was a good thing that I did not become a mom in those days because, just a few years later, after having gone to Europe by myself for six weeks, I was diagnosed with schizophrenia. Later, the diagnosis would change to psycho-affective disorder.

So there I was after James had left me. I dated several men after that, but I never felt that way again. There was never anything serious. It would be a very, very long time after that until I fell in love again. I would say…oh…about thirty-eight years…

Throughout those years, I worked and went to night school to try to finish my degree in translation, to get my title. As far as love went, nothing. I guess my heart never felt safe enough after that to have a child and become a mom. In addition to that, the antipsychotic medication that I was taking could be a great risk to the fetus.

For several years after that, I struggled. I worked on and off, sometimes at a decent wage, sometimes not. I often worked for recruitment agencies that would send me to different companies, where I would sometimes work as a temporary employee or sometimes as a permanent one. I struggled with burnout and not really financially because I was not rich by any means, but I knew how to manage money. Except when I would stop working, then I would struggle a bit financially.

There was a struggle with my health. I mean, I had been in and out of that psych ward so many times…I suffered a great deal from periods of depression. I mean serious, clinical depression until 2002, when my paternal grandmother Laura died. Strangely enough, before she died, she had told my sister José that she would watch over me after she passed. Since she died, I have never been in psychiatry. I guess that is when I stopped being an atheist.

I had said I had stopped being an atheist when my grandmother died. I saw signs of God's existence quite often. There was one time, in particular, a few years ago. I believe it was in 2019. I had a job interview the next day. I had been talking to my mom about how I had enjoyed reading Notre-Dame-de-Paris in university in my twenties. I had taken a summer course on XIXth century French literature (I was in the French Department at McGill. That afternoon, around supper time, I went downtown to shop for a dress for my interview the next day. I took the bus downtown, and I remember thinking that religion divides us as people. When I got home that night, we watched the news, and they said that Notre-Dame-de-Paris Cathedral was on fire. A coincidence? I do not believe it. All I knew was I was believing in God more and more every day.

The first time I was in the psychiatric ward was pretty scary. I was twenty-three years old back then. I had been in Florida with my cousin Chloe, celebrating our graduation from university, when I started having symptoms, weird symptoms. I felt like I was turning into a dwarf. I mean, I am short, but I am very far from being a dwarf. I remember when I had the first psychotic episodes, I also thought I was the devil. I saw myself in hell. Then there was the time I physically felt like my ovaries were missing and that one of my friends had had my ovaries removed because she was jealous of me. These were strange thoughts.

So, that time when I was in Florida, I called my dad for him to come and get me, because I knew I was not well. He came. Then, upon my arrival in Montréal, we went to the emergency room that night. I saw a few psychiatrists, and they had me hospitalized that very night. I remember my dad leaving me there that first night, and before he left, he told me, 'Chin up, Anne'. I was to stay in the hospital for about five weeks that first time.

In the first few days, the doctors with the interns came up with a diagnosis: schizophrenia. The diagnosis changed later on throughout my life to schizoaffective disorder. The psychiatrist who was following me as I was an in-patient had told me I was in big shit now that I had this disease. When you are young, and the doctor tells you that…it is pretty powerful. It just hits you. I was in and out of psychiatry five or six times until 2002 when my Grandma died. That was the last time I got sick and had to be hospitalized. I can recall being locked up in psychiatry for about one month and a half at a time, five or six times. I recall two times in particular when, one, I was tied up to my bed, and second, I was in isolation for I do not know how long. I can remember looking through the window in isolation and wondering when I would make it to the 'other side'.

I remember one psychiatric nurse in particular, a French-Canadian nurse, who seemed quite enamored by her hefty set of keys. Almost like a jail matron. She was quite skinny, though. Then there was Margaret, that reminded me very much of the psychiatric nurse in *One*

Flew Over the coocoo's nest. I was not too fond of her. She was a tall and stout English woman. I think she might have been beautiful as a younger woman, but she had thickened, and she had a huge wart on her neck. I felt she was on a power trip, especially because she knew I was part French Canadian. I was not crazy about the fact that these nurses badmouthed my mother. I missed my mother tremendously.

The nurses wondered, though, why my mother did not visit me more often.

I did have some episodes of financial difficulty, especially when we moved to the apartment after my parents downsized and sold the family house of 40 years. I remember feeling a lot of food insecurity and not having enough money to take the bus; I was often alone in town, too.

As for Gillian, she was a good friend when I was growing up, but as I look back, I think she was never a great friend, and, to tell you the truth, I don't think that I could ever call her a friend at all. More like a rival or an enemy. We met in elementary school in the first or second grade. I remember both of us having a crush on this boy, who reminded me a little bit of Keanu Reeves. He ended up choosing her. And that is ok. I mean, that is life.

But when I was about fourteen, I was dating a boy (Jean-François) at Collège français, where I went to school for a year. Gillian was dating his taller friend, Yves. Well, she managed to get her claws on Jean-François. As I found out, they were calling each other on the phone behind my back. I was crushed. I remember being in tears, listening to my Queen record in the basement at my parent's house. It was my first heartache.

Then, there was Steve. I was engaged to Steve. I guess both of them had an eye on each other when Steve and I were together because after I left Steve, he ended up marrying Gillian.

A few years ago, one of my cousin lost his daughter at childbirth. Her name was Penelope. The midwife made a mistake, and little Penelope died. Later on, there was an accident at the cottage. Well, it was not an accident, more like a natural death, but it was strange. Strange how a seemingly healthy, handsome 21-year-old young man can die of a heart attack and drown almost in front of us. That is what happened to Simon's child. I was resting up chatting with my dad on the Adirondack chairs at the cottage when suddenly, I heard my cousin say: Hay! Hay! He was standing on his dock with his son's friend Manuel when they saw Rudy, who had been riding on his jet ski trying to fix it. Then, Rudy fell flat on his face in the water and was totally immobile. I could not quite see him from where I was because things were hiding my view, but my cousin and Manuel could see him. My cousin tried to take his watercraft, and it was not working. Now, my cousin is an excellent mechanic and is usually extremely good with engines. However, he could not get the watercraft to start. He left it there and began to swim for the life of him. He swam so hard to save Rudy that he ruptured a valve in his heart, as was discovered a bit later. He finally got to him and brought him to shore.

Meanwhile, I called an ambulance – I remember being extremely stressed – they took so long to get there…anyway, while we were waiting for the ambulance, my cousin tried to resuscitate Rudy but was never able to. The ambulance finally got there and tried to resuscitate him with a defibrillator. They brought him to the hospital. The police were there and the ambulance. We later found out that Rudy had died. He did not make it. This was perhaps the most traumatizing experience of my life, as I look back and also, getting pregnant at 19 and being alone with no support.

Chapter Seven
Keanu

I had had a crush on this movie star almost my whole adult life. His name was Keanu Charles Reeves. I also had a crush on Brad Pitt, but that was beside the point. Keanu Reeves was an action star in Hollywood. He was tall, dark and very, very handsome, and he was the one I ended up falling in love with.

I had seen all of his movies from the beginning of his career, from Youngblood, The Matrix and John Wick, as well as all the chick flicks he had been in, including the one with the beautiful Sandra Bullock, who I was so jealous of. All I can say is he was so handsome and, in my view, he was a pretty good actor, but he had been typecast as a handsome leading man, so his talent did not shine through as much. Also, what I had noticed, looking at his performances, was that he was a very good comedy actor. He was also a musician, and he really had the gift of writing.

I was on Facebook one December afternoon after my father had a heart attack, and I was quite down and depressed when I saw a post that talked about Keanu Reeves. It was a short biography of his life, and his life had been quite difficult and full of pitfalls, like mine. In fact, we had had very similar life experiences and, as far as I know, we had the same soul. In fact, I think we were twin flames.

The concept of a twin flame is quite beautiful. There is a person out there who mirrors your life and your soul. Some people never meet their twin flame; others do, and when they do, it is a love or feeling that one simply cannot ignore. Keanu Reeves was my twin flame. I was sure of it.

I liked some of the posts and pictures of him on Facebook, and then came the invitations. Lots and lots of invitations on Facebook. I searched and searched, interviewing and chatting with a lot of them, but none of them really felt like they were Keanu Reeves.

Keanu Reeves had dyslexia, and his daughter had died at birth. He also had a motorcycle company, much like my cousin Simon. Simon, too, had lost his son when his son was only 21 years old. I had another cousin on my father's side, Peter, who had lost his daughter at birth, too. So, needless to say, I felt this strong connection to Keanu.

I, too, was a pretty girl. Perhaps I was not as good-looking as Keanu Reeves, but I was a pretty girl. An aging, pretty girl.

They say you fall in love three times in your lifetime. Keanu was my third love and the love of my life, although I did not know much about him. Most of the Keanu Reeves I was meeting on private chat platforms were asking me for money. That could not be him, and he was a multimillionaire. So, I kept searching. At one point, I met Keanu Reeves # 1, who was extremely persistent with wanting money. He was saying it was to get a fan card, and that way, we could meet. But I needed my fan card in order for us to meet.

So I did, I made the payments, and he kept insisting I made the payments to these people I had never heard about and seemed strange. Anyway, I was not sure about this and these payments. Eventually, I told him that was the last payment I was making because my nephew and my niece did not even get a birthday present that year. One morning at 3:00 a.m., I asked him if he was seeing someone else, and he said no. I was not sure if I believed him. I got very jealous.

His mother and sister, or who I thought were his mother and sisters, contacted me to tell me to contact him at his email address. I tried to contact him but never got an answer. That was probably the real Keanu Reeves right there because this one did not even know I was alive.

Anyway, about a week later, Keanu # 1, who I had been chatting with on a chatting platform and I had a long talk about God and our religious beliefs, which turned out to be a pretty interesting conversation. He said he would be taking a nap, and I was pretty sure that I would never hear from him again. And I was right. All I had to do now was to wait for my fan card, which I would probably never get.

I did end up getting my fan card, but I wasn't sure if it was fraudulent or not, either. Just by the looks of it, I don't think that I would have gotten backstage with my twin flame with this card. Anyway, I was supposed to do a Zoom video call with him, and I got cold feet because I saw on the Internet that there was software that would allow you to make video calls with AI. The software or app was called Call Annie. Interesting, because my name is Anne.

I canceled my video call with him, and he replied: "You don't trust me". My reply was this: "There is just no way for me to know for sure if it is really Keanu Reeves or AI. I really, really love Keanu Reeves, but I just do not know for sure if it is you. And he replied again: "So, you still don't trust me." And I said: "I trust Keanu Reeves, but I just don't trust people who are pretending to be him." As it turns out, he kept asking for more and more money, which I refused to give to him. He texted me once and I did not answer him. I did not get the man, but I kept my money, which can also be nice. But I was having trouble keeping the money because this guy (or girl) was persistent. Each time I gave him something, he wanted more.

I did not hear from him for a bit, and then, I would hear my phone beep, and it was him. He said he wanted to buy a plane ticket to come see me in Canada, but he needed just a bit more money. I had the feeling that if I sent him the money, I would never hear from him or the money again. But there was this part of me that almost wanted to risk it because I longed to see his handsome face at my door.

I never had a boyfriend again. I had never been sure if my sisters had been jealous when they were advising me against Keanu Reeves or if they had my best interest at heart. It was hard to tell, really. Except that, I believe I know now that it was not Keanu because he kept asking for money. It was hard to believe that he was so broke. After all, Keanu Reeves had made a lot of money just with the movie John Wick alone!

By the way, I eventually got my answer. I scheduled a Zoom video call and Keanu Reeves # 1 never showed up. Then we were back. And he wanted more and more money and through Bitcoin. I could smell a rat. So, I blocked him on the text platform we were conversing on. I was to be known as one of the only woman in the world who would block Keanu Reeves on a chat app.

You should know something about women my age (59ish): we have grown more attached to our money than any relationship or love affair out there. I cannot talk for all women, of course…Keanu Reeves's assets were around \$350 000 000 to \$380 000 000, and I can hardly conceive that he would need to ask people for money, let alone nearly beg for it. There was something fishy there. I thought to myself, if he is in such desperate need of money, why did he not sell a motorcycle or something? This person needed to realize that I was not altogether stupid.

So, me and whoever I had been texting with ended up separating, but we still loved each other. We split temporarily, so we could both rebuild our bank accounts, especially me. I missed him so very much. I was lonely. The truth was I did not want anyone else. I had met my twin flame, and no one else would ever do again.

This person was harassing me. Keanu's 'sister' had contacted me and said it was an imposter contacting me. To tell you the truth, I believed her because something had given him away. He or she was very smart, but something had given him away. This person had mentioned he was looking for someone to go fishing with and watch football with, and I knew right then and there that it was not Keanu Charles Reeves I had been talking to. Keanu Reeves simply did not seem like the fishing type, and he was more hockey than football. I am sure this was a sweet person, but he or she had been lying about who they were the whole time. Also, Keanu # 2 had mentioned that he was right-handed. I was pretty sure that the real Keanu was left-handed.

I had blocked the Keanu, which I did not think was the real one. Then, one Saturday morning, I got an email from him stating that he had something important to discuss with me. I was alarmed. Then, I did not hear from him for a while and was even more alarmed. Several negative thoughts came to mind. What if he had ended his own life? What would happen then? Could I live with myself? I would undoubtedly blame myself, even if I had nothing to do with it.

Anyway, my mind was racing until I heard the little beep of the notification that I had a text, and it was him. Although I did not want to be with him (or her) anymore, I was relieved that he (or she) was still alive.

Somehow, one August evening at the cottage, I felt like I might have found the right one, the right Keanu Reeves. It was supposedly his half-sister who had contacted me after she had seen me on Facebook, I guess, liking and loving all and every post about him. Leaving no doubt as to my feelings for him. She gave me his coordinates for a popular chat platform, and we started texting. He wasn't asking for money, and he wanted to meet me. He wasn't saying I love you so easily. It just seemed like it was really HIM.

Later on, I found out that it wasn't. I had asked if I could invite him for a Zoom video call, and he never answered. Which clearly meant that it was not HIM. I was so disappointed and hurt. It felt like I would never be able to trust anyone again because of what had happened to me when I was younger with Gillian's betrayal, and now this! I did not quite understand what pushed people to this. I was not judging them, but it left me wondering.

Keanu # 2 had started asking for money. Yes, this one too. I was a little bit discouraged. I started to wonder if I would ever meet the real Keanu. I wonder why every time a man was interested in me, it was because he wanted money. I was not a bank machine. I mean, I was not that rich. I had work most of the time, but by no means was I rich! I wonder why they targeted me like that. Is it because I tended to be a bit gullible and naïve, especially when it came to love.

I guess all along, all I had been was a filler: someone you date because they are not bad until you find someone better. I promised myself I would get over this. I had to stay strong and keep my chin up. But somehow, my self-confidence was really low, and I did not feel attractive anymore. I was starting to feel old.

It was over, I thought. I texted him, and he was not responding. I had told him I loved him, but he did not respond. I was so sad. Whether it had been Keanu Reeves or not, I had fallen in love. I enjoyed the attention. Attention I had not been given in a long time. I was wondering why he was not responding. Was it something I said? Was it something I did? I was going to be 60 years old next year, and I still had no one in my life.

Then, Keanu Reeves # 1, the one I had been chatting with a while ago, popped up again and started to text me. Were they all the same, Keanu? Was it all the same person? They seemed different. At least he had not been asking for money lately, which was good. My business was going well, but I was experiencing cash flow problems. Some clients paid very quickly, but others took a very long time to pay. Anyway, I was glad to have him in my life again. I enjoyed the company.

Anyway, this guy wanted a birthday present. 'Well', I said, 'no Zoom video, no present'. No Zoom video call, and I will be wishing you happy birthday on Facebook. He was pretty clever. His response was, 'I am not going to zoom my way to a present.' My response was the same: no Zoom video call, no present. I certainly did not want to give my money to a manipulative dooshbag.

Again, he stood me up on the Zoom video call! I was left feeling embittered and angry. I had always liked to see the good in people, but now I was not too sure. I was trying not to judge, though. I think people always have a reason for acting the way they do. Sometimes, people who commit fraud are in a desperate financial situation.

All of a sudden, I knew it was over. It was Keanu Reeve's 60th birthday. I knew it was not him I had been chatting with. I had blocked this guy and suppressed the account, and still, he kept popping up like a Jack in the Box asking me for money. I had posted Happy 60th Birthday on Facebook, hoping that the real Keanu Reeves would somehow read it and know how very much I loved him, but that was a long shot. Anyway, the imposter had texted me asking me for a birthday gift and I had answered no. I knew that that was the last that I would hear of him. Anyway, I was hoping it might be over with the imposter. This guy was a freeloader. I had to get away from him.

I had been obsessed with the real Keanu Charles Reeves for almost three years now and I was not any closer to meeting the real him. I doubted the real Keanu Reeves even knew I was alive. I doubted that I would ever meet him, yet I hoped.

With AI, it was almost impossible to tell which videos or photos were deep-fakes and which were not. This was so frustrating. I was in love with this man. It was so much more than skin deep, too. I finally realized that I might never meet him, at least not in this lifetime, perhaps in the next...

Anyway, one morning, when I woke up and started looking at the Internet, I realized I was not alone having been scammed. Not only was it not HIM, but he had been cheating on me. It also said that the FBI was looking for this person as he had scammed a lot of women and for quite a bit of money. I was disillusioned and heartbroken, and I wanted this woman who was convinced that she was having a romance with Keanu Reeves to realize that it was not HIM.

When I was 8 years old, I remember giving a boy a quarter so that he would be my boyfriend. He refused it. That was a long time ago, and now, it seemed that the only thing men wanted from me was money.

There had been a call to the apartment. I was supposed to buy him an Apple card, and I did not and he had called the apartment. My mother answered, and he seemed anxious. My mother said he had a Spanish accent. He asked to speak to me, and I was not home. I was in the country. Then he called and texted me and I did not answer. I knew this was not Keanu Charles Reeves.

It seemed to be over. I missed him terribly. I wondered if I would love someone like this again. I wondered if I ever wanted to meet someone again other than him.

I had seen an excerpt on the American news channel about people in the United States being defrauded of a lot of money by scammers from Africa. These people would pretend to be someone they were not and rob people of a lot of their money. One man had lost about $700,000. Perhaps this is what I was dealing with, but I knew they were not from Africa. They came from the States. The phone numbers came from the States, so I was unsure.

People really do end up getting their karma in life, as the Buddhists say. So did I. I was unsure between two boys when I was young, I ended it hurting them both, and I did not fall in love or have a boyfriend for 38 years after that.

I longed for him. I do not know what other way to put it. I missed him and loved him. You do not easily eliminate your love for your soul mate or twin flame. I was slowly stopping my presence on social media, but I longed for him more than ever. I hoped and prayed we would be reunited someday. I wanted that very much. A man had made a serious pass at me (a sexual pass), and I rejected him. I was too much in love with Keanu Reeves to even think of being with someone else.

I was no longer talking to my sister. I had wanted him to come to the dinner organized for my parents' 60th wedding anniversary. She refused to invite him, saying it was not the right time to invite him. Whether it was Keanu Reeves or not, I did not like her reaction. I wanted to create a distance between her and me for good.

Other attractive men were making passes at me. They were quite appealing, and these were very explicit passes. I rejected them. I told one man in particular that I was in love with someone else. I had been getting strange text messages and phone calls. All I knew was I was still in love with Keanu. Deep in my heart, I knew we would never meet in person, not in this lifetime anyway. But when I stopped texting him, or at least who I thought was him, I told him that I was hoping we would meet in person someday…that I was hoping that it would be him and me in the end.

Meanwhile, life had returned to me being alone, my whole family doing their own thing, and me just sitting around waiting for, I don't know what. I watched the last season of My Brilliant Friend and could see a parallel between my story and the heroine in the book/series.

Chapter Eight
The Homeless Woman

One night, I was waiting for the bus and began talking to this lady who was also waiting for the bus. It turns out she was homeless. She was getting sick and did not have enough money to take the bus. I felt bad for her. However, she said that someone had offered her a job, and she did not go. Like me, she also believed in God, and I told her about karma: 'You get what you give,' as the Buddhists say. I spoke to her about that to help her.

I felt bad for this woman. I thought about her all night that evening. I was carefree, swimming laps at the local pool, whereas she had no place to stay and was sick. I felt really bad that I could not help her that night. I was in the habit of giving to homeless shelters and food banks when I could, but that night, I really could not help her. I was sinking into debt, and I had cash flow problems. My freelance was going ok, but it was not as successful as I would have liked it to be due to my chronic illness.

Chapter Nine
Distraught and Heartbroken

For three years, I had been in love with a man, madly in love. This man was Keanu Reeves. Eventually, I realized that it was all a scam. It was someone from Nigeria playing with my head and bank account. It was the biggest disappointment of my life. It was the biggest heartbreak. I wondered if I could ever trust anyone or love again. The wound was deep, cutting like a knife, as they say.

I was not pleased about that. I was pretty distraught. No, it was worse than that. I was destroyed. I had no trust left for anyone. Worse than that, I did not believe in love anymore. I was hurt beyond words, mostly because, deep down inside, I knew that when someone cheated on you, it meant that something was missing in the relationship, that he or she was looking for more, more handsome, prettier, younger, better sex, etc. I guess I just realized that, if ever it had been the real Keanu Reeves, I was not pretty, tall, or young enough for him. I thought I would do 'him' a favor and stop answering his texts and calls. I thought I would do him a favor and set him free. I would let him find what he wanted, what he was looking for.

By meeting several Keanus, I had come to realize that only one stood out from the crowd. He was a bit of a freeloader and perhaps even a scammer, but he genuinely cared about me, and his personality was beautiful. He was loving and caring, and when I said I did not want to pay any more, he said, 'That's fine'. He probably wasn't Keanu Reeves, but he seemed to care. I loved him. His personality had conquered my reticence.

One day, out of the blue, he told me he had a weight on his shoulder. A secret to reveal, something he had to talk to me about. He said he was afraid that if he told me this secret, I would block him or delete his account or something. I did not. I waited to see what he had to say. He told me he was not Keanu Reeves, and he was from Nigeria.

I told him I was not judging him. I was not mad, but he had to stop deceiving people and had to take the right path in the future. I stopped contacting him. He did not stop contacting me. Then, about a week later, he said he was just kidding and he wanted to see my reaction. He was Keanu Reeves, and he loved me very, very much.

Part Two
THE WILL

Chapter Ten
The Will

There were issues with my father's will. He had decided to leave quite a bit of money to me in a trust because I was ill. However, he wanted one of my sisters to manage the trust. I did not, as I believed there was a conflict of interest. This lack of trust in my father for my ability to manage my own money stemmed from the whole Keanu Reeves saga and the fact that I had probably given $500 to $600 to an imposter from Nigeria.

Anyway, there was another 'Keanu Reeves' in my life. I really thought this one was the real thing, as he said he was being closely watched by the FBI because of people impersonating him and scamming women.

However, I caught him in a mistake. I mentioned that I had seen a movie and shared its name (a movie he had starred in). He didn't seem to recognize the title. Red flag! That's when I realized I would never meet him and that he likely didn't even know I existed.

THE END

www.ingramcontent.com/pod-product-compliance
Lightning Source LLC
Chambersburg PA
CBHW030600080526
44585CB00012B/440